The symbols in the book tell you whether the animal is:

Vertebrate ■ or invertebrate □
Warm blooded ▲ or cold blooded △
Nocturnal ▬ or diurnal ▭
and whether the animal has babies (young born alive) ● or lays eggs ○

If there is no symbol ▬ or ▭ it means that the animal sometimes sleeps in the day and sometimes at night.

Scientists classify animals into groups.
The animals in this encyclopaedia fit into the following groups:

mollusc	crustacean	arachnid
insect	fish	amphibian
reptile	bird	mammal

Some of the words you may not understand are explained in the glossary on page 70 in Volume 4.

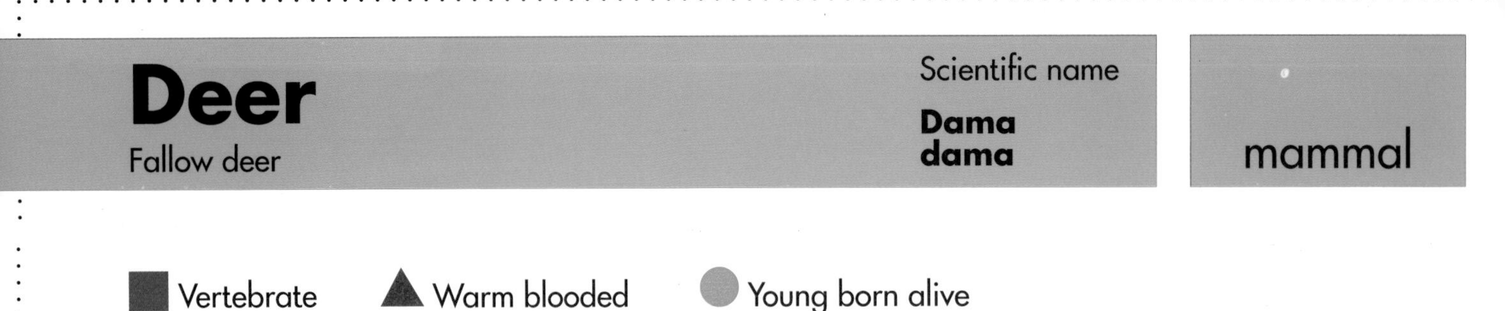

Deer

Fallow deer

Scientific name

Dama dama

mammal

Vertebrate

Warm blooded

Young born alive

Deer live in herds. The male deer are called bucks. Bucks have antlers. In Autumn bucks sometimes fight each other. They run towards each other and clash antlers.

Home
Woodland, parkland.

Young
One baby (fawn) a year.
Born in June.

Food
Grass, leaves.

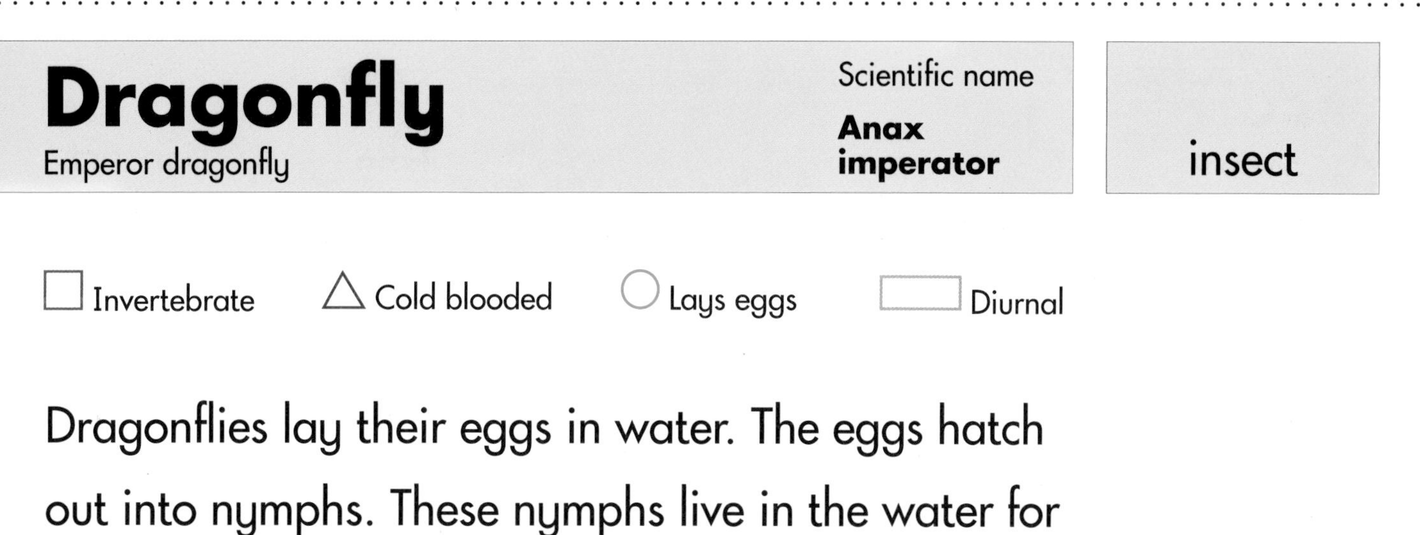

Dragonfly

Emperor dragonfly

Scientific name
Anax imperator

insect

Invertebrate · Cold blooded · Lays eggs · Diurnal

Dragonflies lay their eggs in water. The eggs hatch out into nymphs. These nymphs live in the water for two years. Then they burst out of their skins and fly away. They have turned into dragonflies.

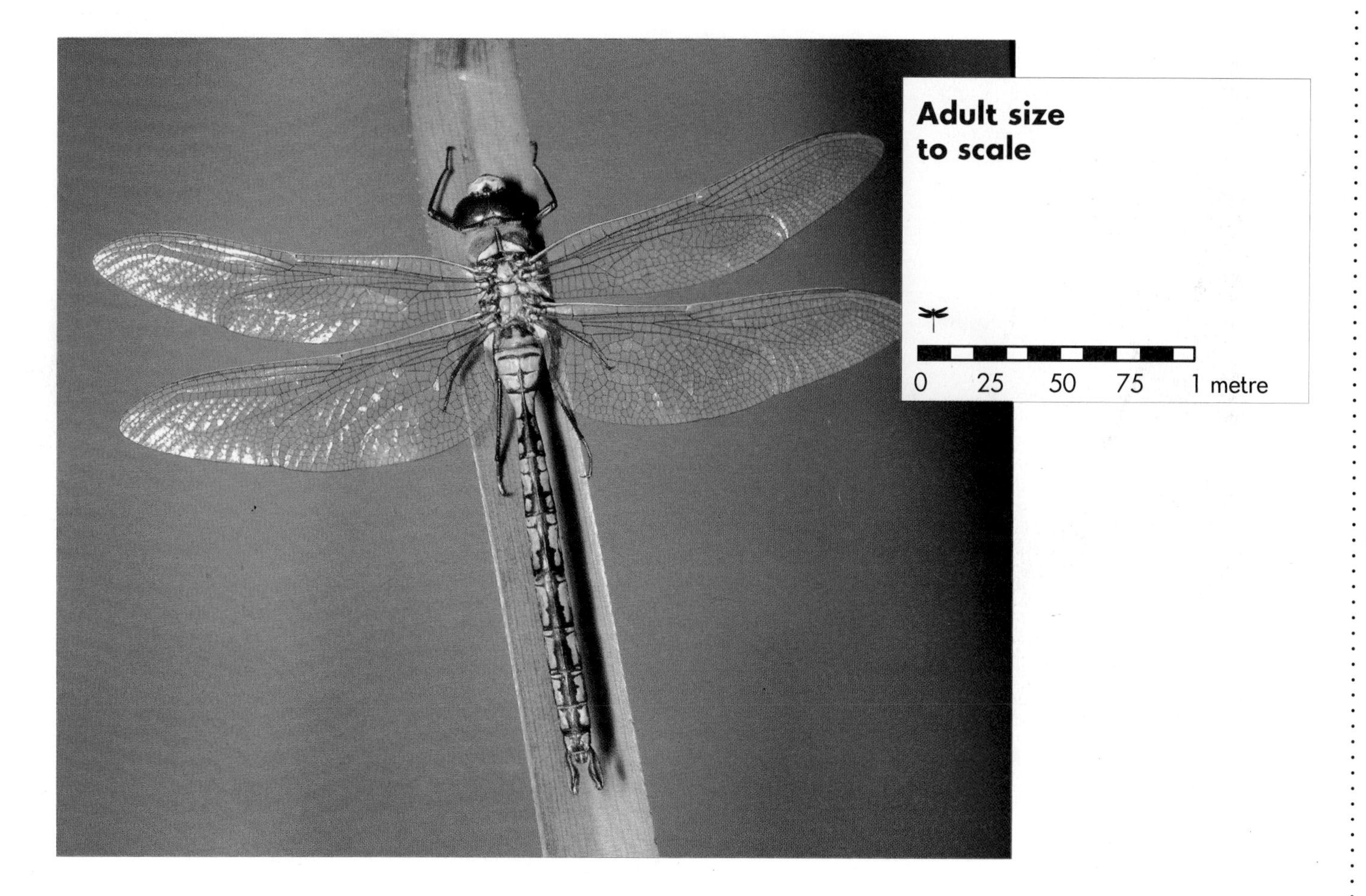

Home
Near ponds and rivers, damp meadows.

Young
Over 100 eggs laid on water. Hatch into nymphs.

Food
Adults eat insects. Nymphs eat tadpoles, small fish.

Earwig

Common earwig

Scientific name

Forficula auricularia

insect

□ Invertebrate △ Cold blooded ○ Lays eggs

Earwigs are common in gardens. They can fly but they prefer to crawl and climb. You often find them under stones and logs. A male earwig has curved pincers but a female has straight pincers.

Actual adult size

Home

Gardens, woodland. In cracks, under logs, stones.

Young

50 yellow eggs laid underground.

Food

Plants, flower petals.

Fox

Scientific name
Vulpes vulpes

mammal

Vertebrate · Warm blooded · Young born alive · Nocturnal

Foxes used to live only in the countryside. Nowadays many of them live in towns where it is easy to find scraps of food. At night you can sometimes hear them barking and wailing.

Home
Open spaces, towns, farms.

Young
4 to 5 babies (cubs) in a litter.

Food
Rabbits, birds, beetles, berries, scraps from bins.

Frog

Common frog

Scientific name

Rana temporaria

amphibian

Vertebrate

Cold blooded

Lays eggs

Frogs can live in or out of water. Female frogs lay eggs (called frogspawn) in water. Tadpoles hatch from the frogspawn. They grow into frogs.

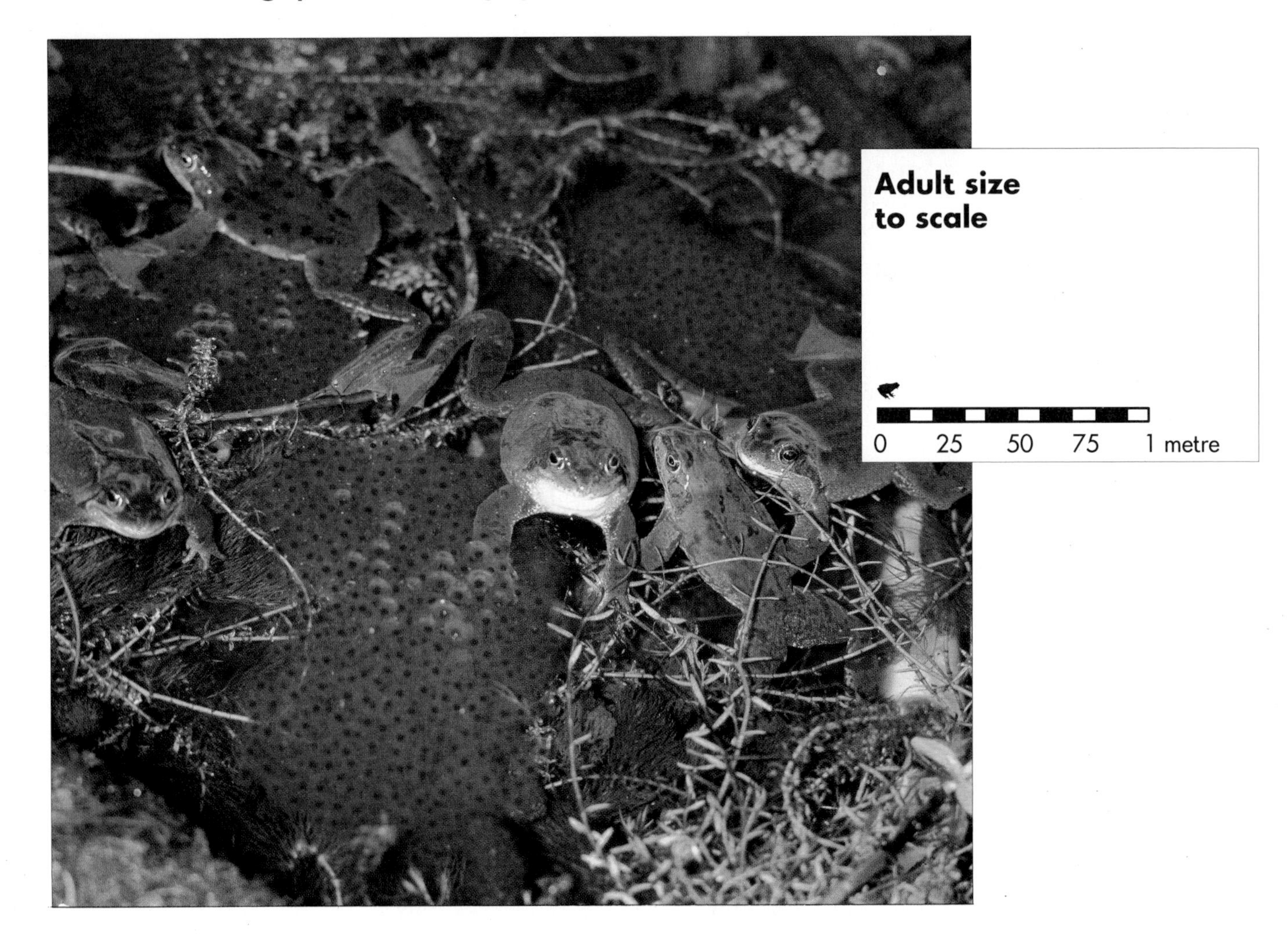

Home
Damp places, banks of rivers, ponds.

Young
Eggs (frogspawn) laid in water . 1000 to 3000 eggs laid.

Food
Insects, grubs, worms.

Grass snake

Scientific name

Natrix natrix

reptile

■ Vertebrate △ Cold blooded ○ Lays eggs ▭ Diurnal

The grass snake is not a poisonous snake but it pretends to bite when it is frightened. If it is attacked it sometimes pretends to be dead. It can also squirt a smelly liquid at its enemies.

Adult size to scale

0 25 50 75 1 metre

Home

Open spaces near water. Damp grass and ditches. Banks of ponds.

Young

30 to 40 white leathery eggs. Laid in piles of leaves and dung heaps.

Food

Frogs, newts, toads, slugs, worms, fish.

Gull

Blackheaded gull

Scientific name

Larus ridibundus

bird

Vertebrate | Warm blooded | Lays eggs | Diurnal

Gulls are sea birds but they can be seen almost anywhere. They are called scavengers because they will eat almost anything. Blackheaded gulls only have black heads in the Summer. For the rest of the year their heads are white.

Home
Seaside, farmland, rubbish tips.

Young
3 grey eggs with brown speckles.

Food
Almost anything, even rubbish.

Hare

Brown hare

Scientific name

Lepus europaeus

mammal

■ Vertebrate ▲ Warm blooded ● Young born alive

Hares look like rabbits but they have longer ears and they run instead of hopping. In Spring they seem to go mad. They stand on their back legs and box each other. Then they run around the fields.

Home
Fields and farmland. Lives in a form (a dip in the ground).

Young
2 to 3 babies (leverets) in a litter.

Food
Plants. Also eats its own droppings

Hedgehog

Scientific name
Erinaceus europaeus

mammal

Vertebrate ▲ Warm blooded ● Young born alive Nocturnal

The hedgehog is a spiky animal. It can roll up into a sharp ball to protect itself. The hedgehog hibernates in Winter but when the weather is warmer it sometimes wakes up and looks for food.

Adult size to scale

0 25 50 75 1 metre

Home
Woodlands, gardens. Hibernates in piles of leaves.

Young
3 to 5 babies born in July.

Food
Birds' eggs, slugs, snails, insects.

Jay

Scientific name
Garrulus glandarius

bird

Vertebrate · Warm blooded · Lays eggs · Diurnal

The jay is a noisy bird. It likes to eat acorns. It stores these in holes in the ground but sometimes forgets where they are. These forgotten acorns can grow into oak trees.

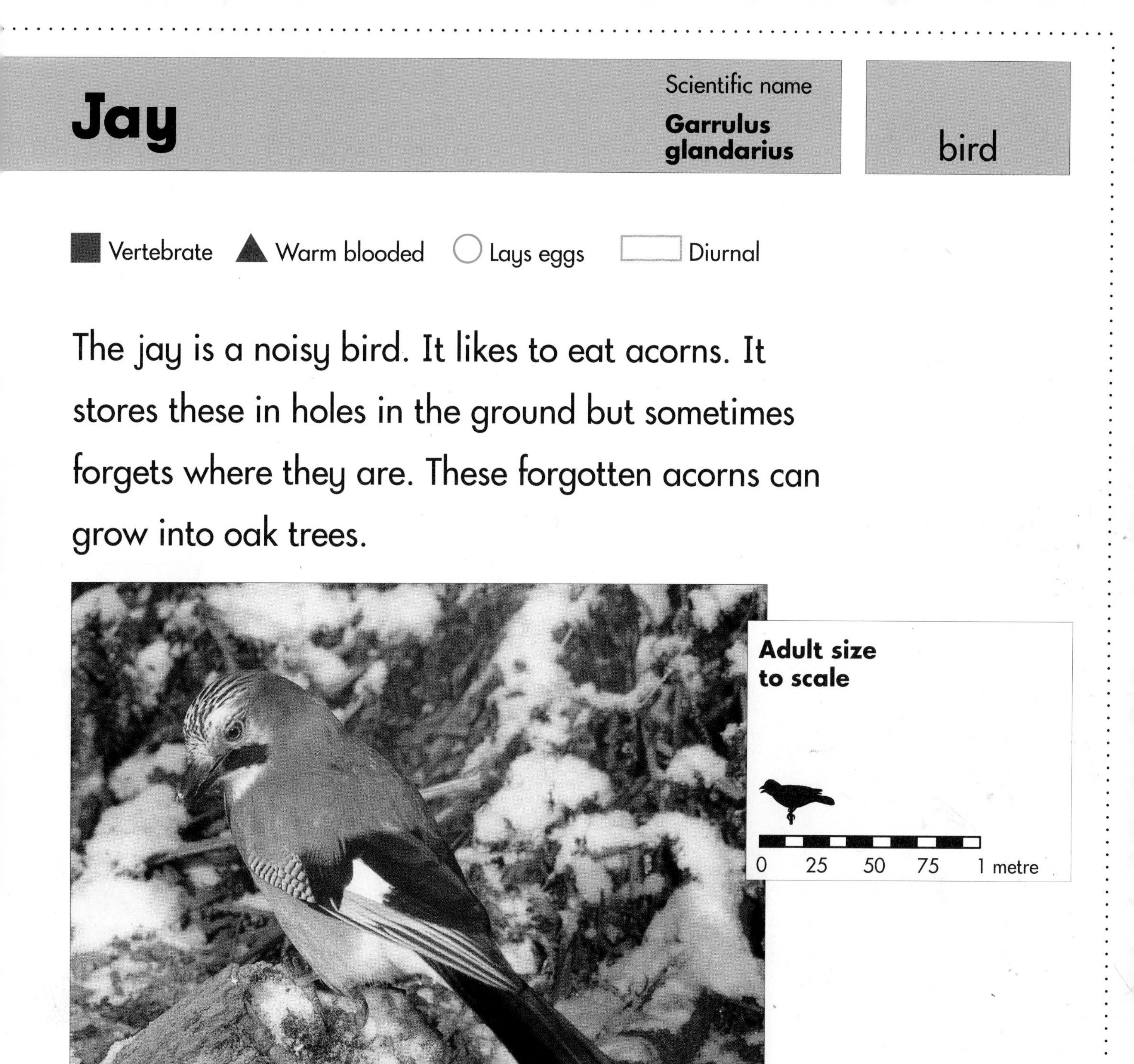

Home
Woodlands, parks, gardens.
Nests in trees.

Young
5 to 7 dull green eggs, with brown specks.

Food
Acorns, nuts, berries, eggs, young birds.

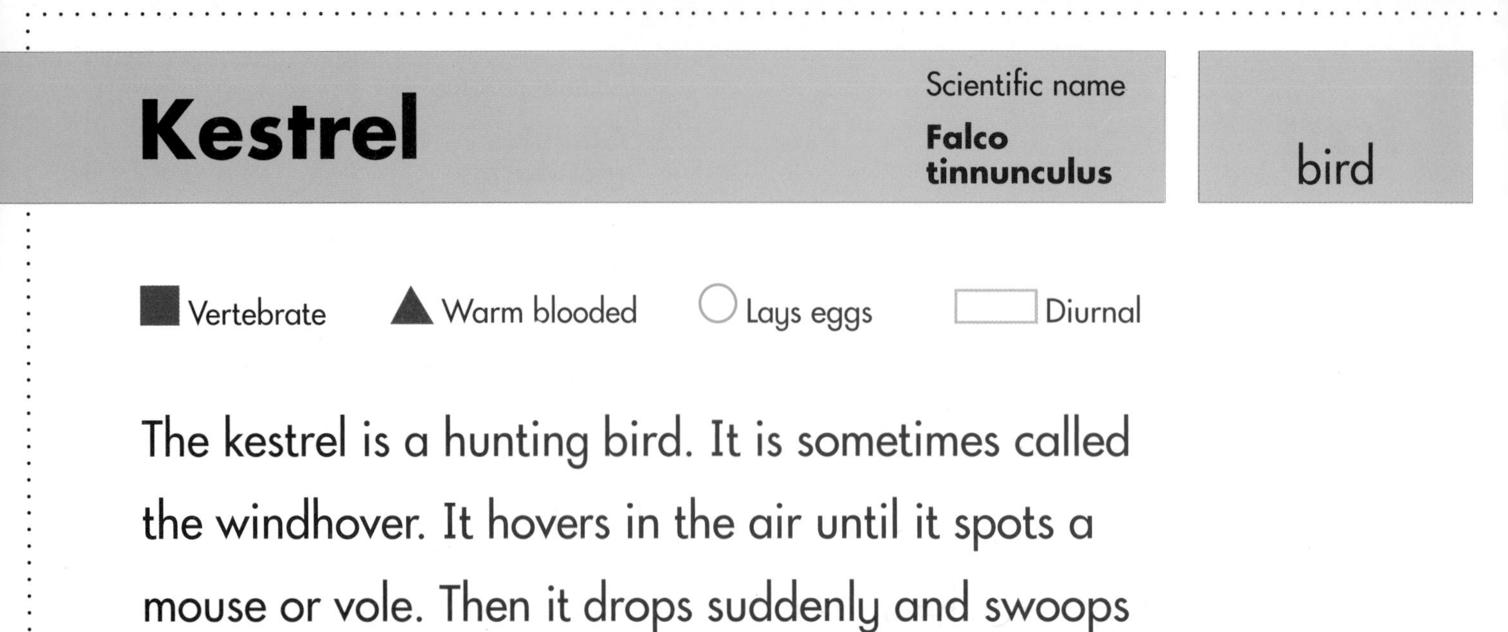

Kestrel

Scientific name
Falco tinnunculus

bird

Vertebrate · Warm blooded · Lays eggs · Diurnal

The kestrel is a hunting bird. It is sometimes called the windhover. It hovers in the air until it spots a mouse or vole. Then it drops suddenly and swoops to catch the prey.

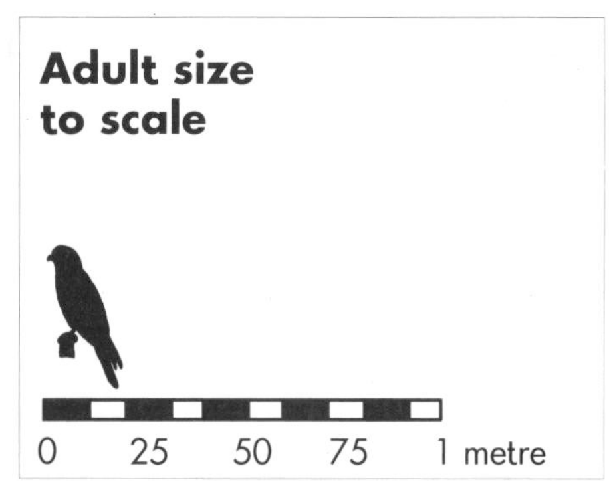

Home
Open land.
Nests in hollow trees.

Young
4 to 5 reddish brown speckled eggs.

Food
Mice, lizards, other small creatures.

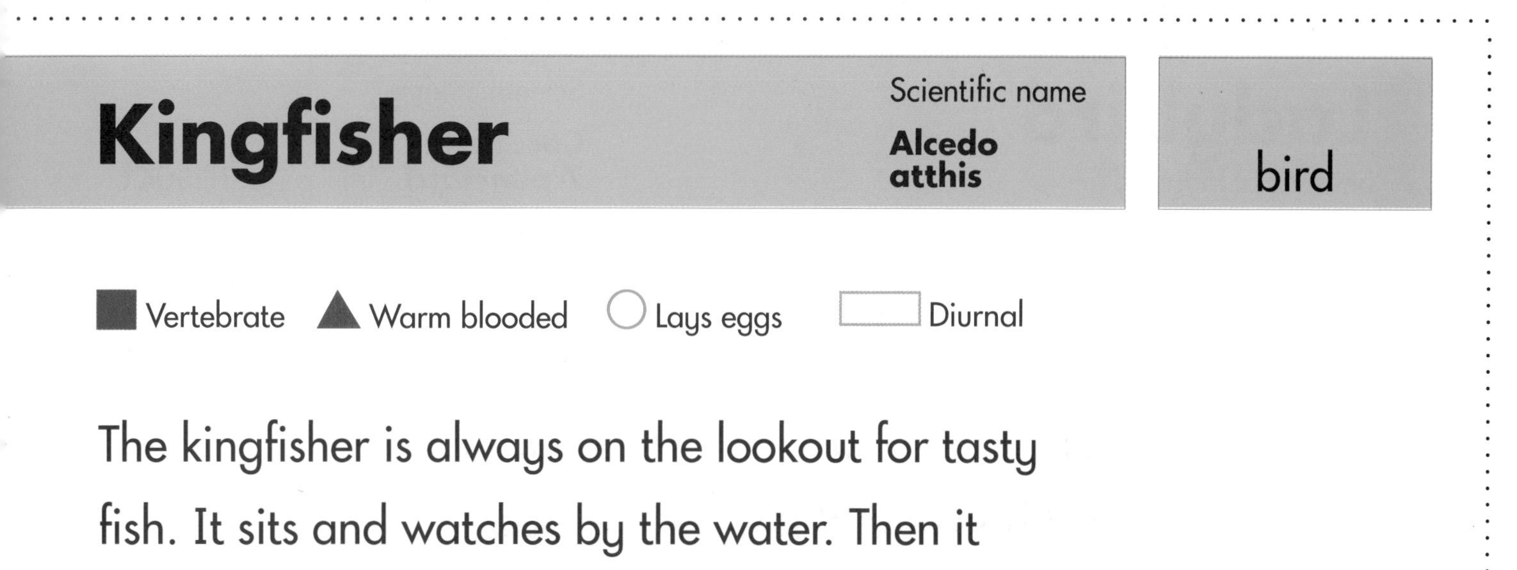

Kingfisher

Scientific name
Alcedo atthis

bird

■ Vertebrate ▲ Warm blooded ○ Lays eggs ▭ Diurnal

The kingfisher is always on the lookout for tasty fish. It sits and watches by the water. Then it plunges headfirst into the water and catches the fish. It swallows the fish in one gulp.

Adult size to scale

0 25 50 75 1 metre

Home
The banks of lakes, ponds, rivers.
Nests in holes it makes in river banks.

Young
5 to 7 glossy eggs laid in a hole in the bank.

Food
Mostly fish.

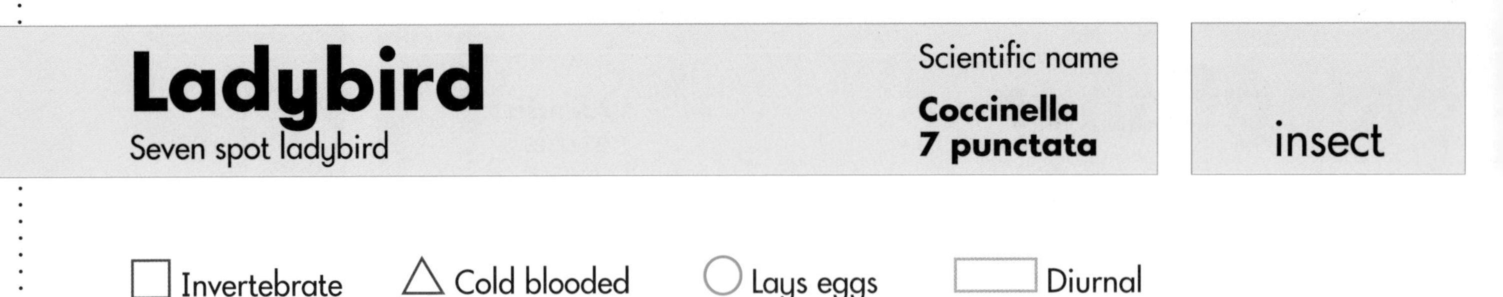

Ladybird

Seven spot ladybird

Scientific name

Coccinella 7 punctata

insect

Invertebrate — Cold blooded — Lays eggs — Diurnal

Ladybirds are helpful to gardeners. They eat the greenfly that harm plants. The bright colours of the ladybird warn birds not to eat it. Its body has poisons in it which could harm birds.

Home
Woodland, meadows, gardens.

Young
About 200 eggs laid on plants.

Food
Greenfly, other small insects.

Limpet

Common limpet

Scientific name

Patella vulgata

mollusc

☐ Invertebrate △ Cold blooded ○ Lays eggs

The limpet has its own special place on a rock near the seashore. It sticks itself to this rock. Every limpet egg hatches into a male limpet. Every male limpet changes to a female limpet when it grows up.

Home
Seashore.
Clings to a rock.

Young
Millions of eggs laid in the sea.

Food
Tiny plants.

Lizard

Common lizard

Scientific name

Lacerta vivipara

reptile

■ Vertebrate △ Cold blooded ○ Lays eggs ▭ Diurnal

Lizards have sharp claws. They cling to walls and rocks. If it is attacked and caught, a lizard can escape by leaving its tail behind. Another tail will grow.

Home
Grassland, meadows, walls and stony places.

Young
5 to 10 eggs.
They hatch as soon as they are laid.

Food
Insects, spiders.